J GN
DISNEY

Walt Disney's Comics and Stories
No. 654, March 2005
Published monthly by Gemstone Publishing,

ISBN 0-911903-79-8

Walt Disney's DONALD DUCK
· BUSYBODIES ·

HEY! LOOK, UNCA DONALD! SOMEONE'S MOVING INTO THE RENTAL NEXT DOOR!

THAT PLACE HAS BEEN EMPTY FOR MONTHS!

2003-011

THAT'S PRETTY ODD LOOKING LUGGAGE HE'S CARRYING!

FUNNY SHAPES FOR SUITCASES!

KIND OF A CREEPY LOOKING GUY, ISN'T HE?

COME ON, NOSY-ROSIES! WHAT THE GUY LOOKS LIKE OR DOES IS NONE OF **OUR** BUSINESS! NOW LET'S GO RUSTLE UP SOME CHOW!

YEAH, BUT WHERE'S HIS **FURNITURE**? ALL HE'S HAULING ARE THOSE FUNNY LOOKING CASES!

IT'S A **FURNISHED** RENTAL! ALL HE NEEDS ARE HIS PERSONAL BELONGINGS! NOW **GIDDIAP!**

PRETTY GOOFY LOOKING **BELONGINGS**, IF YOU ASK ME!

NOBODY ASKED YOU!

However, over the next couple of days, Donald grows increasingly suspicious of the new neighbor!

I'M TELLING YOU, THERE'S SOMETHING **WEIRD** ABOUT THAT GUY!

I THOUGHT HE WAS NONE OF OUR BUSINESS!

YEAH, WELL I'VE CHANGED MY MIND!

IMPROVEMENTS ARE ALWAYS WELCOME!

SEE FOR YOURSELVES! THERE'S AN ODD GIZMO STICKING OUT THROUGH THE CURTAINS OVER THERE!

SO? MAYBE IT'S A TELESCOPE!

MAYBE THE GUY'S AN AMATEUR **ASTRONOMER**!

AND I SUPPOSE WE'RE THE PLANET **NEPTUNE**! HE'S POINTING THAT THING AT **US**!

COOL OFF, UNCA DONALD! YOU'RE GETTING ALL WORKED UP OVER NOTHING!

SEE? NOW IT'S POINTED AT THE **SKY**!

YOU WERE RIGHT THE FIRST TIME! WHAT OUR NEW NEIGHBOR DOES IS **HIS** BUSINESS – NOT **OURS**!

Dear Mr. Mouse,

You are invited to a birthday party in UTMOST SECRECY. Your presence is most dearly wished and urgently needed. DO NOT RSVP. Just BE at Floyd Gardens, 7:30 PM. I will see you — I KNOW —

AT LAST, AS TWO WEEK'S DRAW TO A CLOSE...

LISTEN, GANG! PETE'S *KEPT* GROWING SINCE THE LESSONS WE GAVE HIM -- AND HE'S GROWING UP *RIGHT* THIS TIME!

I MEAN, IT'S LIKE I'M HIS *BIG BROTHER* NOW! AND YOU CAN'T GO WRONG WITH A BIG BROTHER'S HELP!

AND NOW PETE'S *BIRTHDAY* IS COMING UP! I'M THINKING WE SHOULD ALL GO CAMPING TO CELEBRATE IT *AND* HIS *NEW* SELF! WE--

NO, MICKEY!

;HUH?!; WHADDAYA MEAN...

MICKEY, NO! *MAYBE* YOU'VE REFORMED PETE BUT HE'S STILL A *JINX* AROUND *US!*

WHETHER HE'S SIX OR SIXTEEN...

OR EIGHTY-NINE!

OR EIGH-- I MEAN, THINK OF THE *HORRIBLE* THINGS HE'S DONE!

B-BUT THAT WAS... AS HIS *OLD* SELF...

WE'RE SORRY, MICKEY, BUT WE JUST DON'T *TRUST* HIM! AND WE'RE *AFRAID* TO HANG AROUND *YOU* AS LONG AS HE'S WITH YOU!

MICKEY, *WHY* DIDN'T THE GANG WANNA BE WITH US?

NEVER MIND! THEY'LL COME AROUND! I'M SURE THEY...

MINERAL WATER

BEEF

;HMPF!; IF *THEY* DON'T NEED *US*, *WE* DON'T NEED *THEM!*

YEAH, WHAT'S THE BIG DEAL ANYWAY?

SHORTLY...

WE'RE GONNA GO ROWING ON WILD RIVER, PAL-- BY *OURSELVES*! MAYBE WE'LL SET A NEW *SPEED RECORD*!

HECK, YOU'RE STRONG ENOUGH TO SET A RECORD ALONE!

WE'LL BE IMMORTALIZED... RIGHT ON *YOUR* BIRTHDAY! SO LET'S ROW *FASTER* THAN *ANYBODY'S* EVER ROWED!

I DON'T KNOW WHAT'S AROUND THE RIVERBEND! BUT WE'LL ONLY SEE IT IF WE GO... AND *GO* AND--

OMIGOSH!

MICKEY!

CRACK!

WHOA, THAT WAS CLOSE! BE A GOOD GUY AND *PULL ME UP*, HUH, PETE?

IF I *WUZ* A GOOD GUY-- I MIGHT!

AW, PETE! DON'T JOKE ABOUT...

WALT DISNEY presents

Donald Duck

in

FROZEN GOLD

SNOW AND COLD! COLD AND SNOW! I'M **SICK** OF IT!

LET'S GO

DOWN **SOUTH**,

UNCA' DONALD!

IT COSTS TOO MUCH **MONEY** TO GO SOUTH!

MAYBE IF WE SHOVELED

MORE SNOW

AT FIFTY CENTS AN HOUR—

DON'T LET ME HEAR ANYMORE ABOUT **SNOW**! I'LL GO **CRAZY**!

IF WE ONLY HAD THAT **PLANE**, UNCA' DONALD,

WE COULD **GO SOUTH**

IN A HURRY!

FOR SALE

HMF! HOW WOULD I GET A PLANE LIKE THAT — **TRADE MY HOUSE** FOR IT?

SAY, UNCA' DONALD,

THAT'S

AN IDEA!!

YEAH—AND A MIGHTY CRAZY IDEA! WHY, NOBODY BUT A **FOOL** WOULD MAKE A TRADE LIKE THAT!

WONDER HOW FAST THAT PLANE CAN FLY?

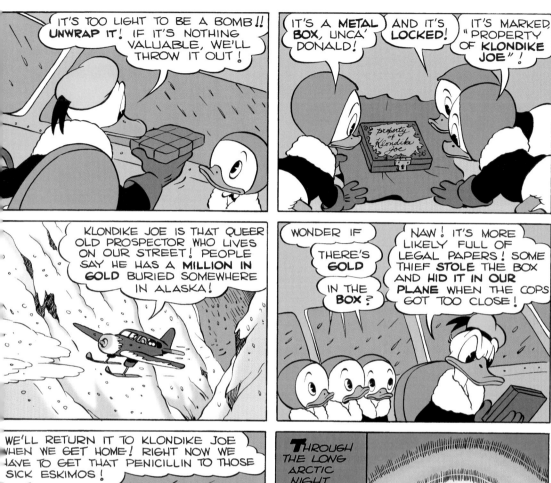

MEANWHILE DONALD'S PREDICAMENT HAS BECOME WORSE! THE GLARE HAS MADE HIM SNOWBLIND, AND HE STRUGGLES ALONG, UNABLE TO SEE A THING!

SURE HAS BEEN A SHORT DAY! IT HAS GOTTEN DARK ALREADY!

LUCKY FOR ME THAT THE SNOW IS ALL LEVEL AROUND HERE!

AND THERE ARE NO LAKES OR THINGS TO FALL INTO!

I HEAR CRUNCHING — LIKE BIG CHUNKS OF ICE RUBBING TOGETHER!

THE DRIFTING FLOES CLOSE THE GAPS AHEAD OF DONALD'S FEET!

THE GROUND SEEMS TO BE MOVING!

BUT IT'S AS EVEN AS A FLOOR!

KINDA SLIPPERY IN SPOTS!

IT'S NICE TO KNOW THAT NO ANIMALS LIVE IN THESE LATITUDES!

MEANWHILE THE KIDS HAVE BEEN DOING THEIR BEST TO ESCAPE FROM THE HOTEL!

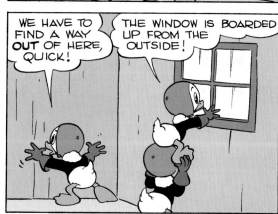

OUR HEROES DELIVER THE CROOKS, CABIN AND ALL, TO THE CONSTABLE AT POINT MARROW! THEN, WITH KLONDIKE JOE'S GOLD ABOARD THEIR PLANE, THEY TURN SOUTH FOR HOME!

WE'RE GLAD YOUR EYES ARE WELL AGAIN, UNCA' DONALD!

AND I'M GLAD TO BE HEADIN' SOUTH — I NEVER WANT TO SEE ANYMORE SNOW AS LONG AS I LIVE!

HOME AGAIN

WOW! LOOK AT THE CROWD! YOU'D THINK WE WERE HEROES FOR FLYIN' THAT PENICILLIN TO THE ESKIMOS!

WELCOME DUCK'S

DONALD DUCK, I PRESENT YOU THE KEY TO THE CITY!

THANKS, MAYOR, BUT WE WILL BE FLYIN' ON SOUT AS SOON AS I DELIVER THIS GOLD TO KLONDIK JOE!

HERE'S KLONDIKE, RIGHT HERE! STEP UP, KLONDIKE, AND TAKE OVER YOUR MILLION DOLLARS!

LADYWIMMIN AN' GINTS, I NEVER EXPECTED TO SEE THIS HERE GOLD AGIN, SO I'M GONNA DO A RIGHT HANDSOME THING WITH IT!

HOORAY!

ATTABOY, KLONDIKE!

YIPPEE KI YI!

I'M GONNA SPEND THE WHOLE MILLION FOR MORE PENICILLIN FOR THESE BRAVE BOYS TO FLY TO MORE SICK ESKIMOS!

GRACIOUS! WHAT COULD HAVE HAPPENE TO THE DUCK'S? ALL FOUR OF THEM FAINTED DEAD AWAY!

12|07